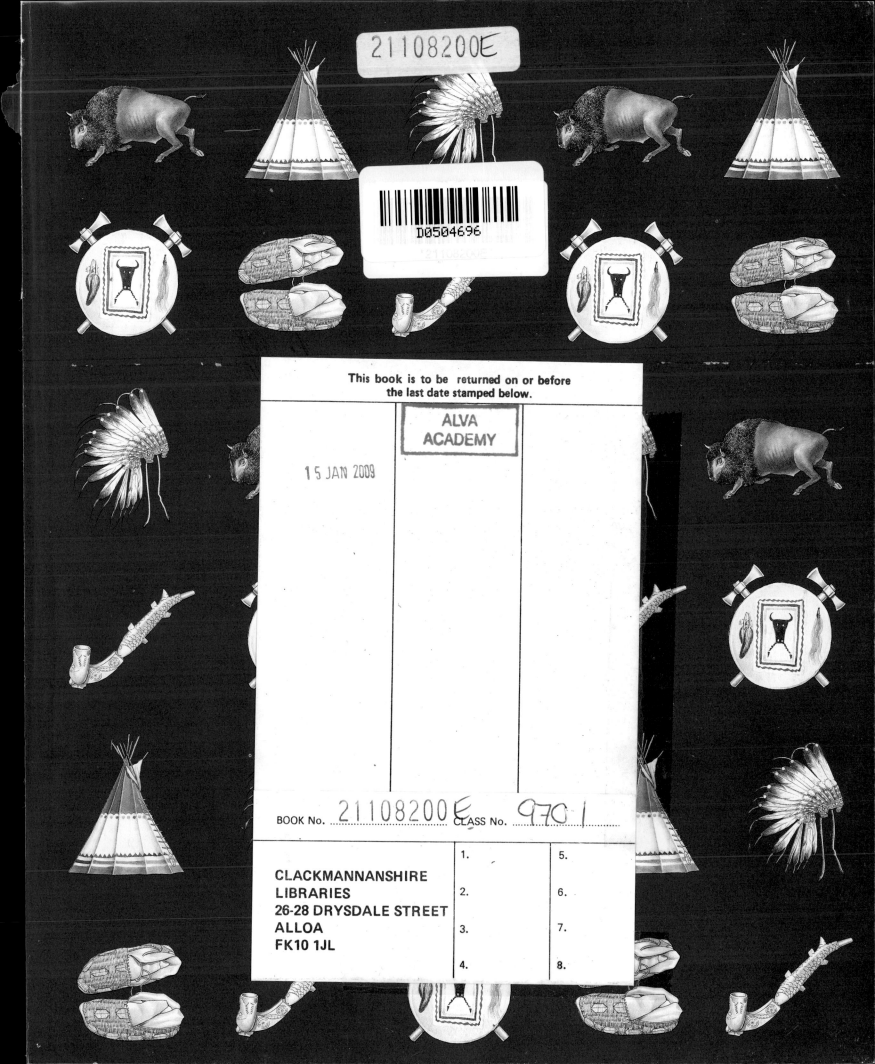

THE PLAINS
INDIANS

ALYS SWAN-JACKSON

Acknowledgements

The author and publishers would like to thank Richard Green and Richard Cupidi for their assistance; Bill Le Fever, who illustrated the see-through pages; and the organizations which have given their permission to reproduce the following pictures:

Provincial Museum of Alberta/H89.220.72; courtesy of the Ethnology Program: 31 top right.
The Anschutz Collection/James O. Milmoe: 39 centre.
Bridgeman Art Library/Alecto Historical Editions/Joslyn Art Museum: 30 top, 34 top left.
British Museum (Museum of Mankind): 26 top.
The Denver Public Library, Western History Department: 11 bottom.
Founders Society Detroit Institute of Arts: 22, 23 top centre, /Buffalo Bill Historical Center, Cody, WY, Chandler-Pohrt Collection 27 top.
The Granger Collection: 9 top, 27 bottom right, 43 top, 44 top left.
Richard Green: 12 top, 37 bottom right.
The Greenwich Workshop, Inc/Transferring the Medicine Shield by Howard Terpning © 1991, The Greenwich Workshop, Inc. reproduced: 28 bottom.
The Heard Museum/Courtesy Indian Arts and Crafts Board, U.S. Department of the Interior: 29 bottom.
Peter Newark's Western Americana: 4 bottom, 7 top, 15 top, 21 top.
Werner Forman Archive: 18 right, 25 top, 39 top right, /British Museum 20 top, /Field Museum of Natural History, Chicago 18 left, /Maxwell Museum of Anthropology, Albuquerque, USA 4 top, /Museum für Volkerkunde, Berlin 8 top, 10 top, 19 centre, 28 top left, /Museum of the American Indian, Heye Foundation, NY, USA 19 top, /Pohrt Collection, Plains Indian Museum, BBHC, Cody, Wyoming, USA 19 bottom, /R.L. Anderson Coll., Plains Indian Museum, BBHC, Cody, Wyoming, USA 14 top.

Illustrators:
Richard Berridge: 29, 30-31, 36-37, 44-45.
Peter Bull: 5, 43.
James Field: cover, 10-11, 11, 38, 39, 46-47.
Ray Grinaway: 14, 15, 20, 21, 23, 36.
Bill Le Fever: 16-17, 24-25, 32-33, 40-41.
Tony Randall: 12, 13, 19, 37.
Mark Stacey: 6, 7, 8, 9, 26-27, 31.
Simon Williams: 34, 35,42.

In memory of my husband, Robert Joseph Jackson 1945-1990.

Editor: Andrew Farrow
Designer: Mark Summersby
Picture Researcher: Liz Fowler
Production Controller: Linda Spillane and Mark Leonard

First published in Great Britain 1995
by Hamlyn Children's Books,
an imprint of Reed Children's Books,
Michelin House, 81 Fulham Road, London SW3 6RB,
and Auckland, Melbourne, Singapore and Toronto.

Copyright © 1995 Reed International Books Limited.

ISBN 0 600 58415 1

A CIP catalogue record for this book is available at the British Library.

Books printed and bound by Proost, Belgium

CONTENTS

Archaeological remains, such as this flint tool found in New Mexico, and the fossilized bones of bison, date the migrations of the first American peoples somewhere between 30,000 and 10,000 BC.

The peoples of the Plains are probably the best known of all the American Indians. Their feather headdresses and war paint, their tipis and their customs and rituals, as well as their bitter conflict with white settlers, have been described in countless books and films. Many of these accounts have portrayed a romantic and often inaccurate picture. So who were the North American Plains Indians, and what is their history?

EARLY HISTORY

People had lived in North America for thousands of years before the arrival of white European settlers. These very first Americans came to the Americas from Asia, more than 20,000 years ago. During the last Ice Age, the continents of Asia and North America were not separate, as they are today, but joined by a thin strip of land that people could walk across.

GREAT MIGRATIONS

The people who crossed into North America were nomads, following the animals that they hunted. They also gathered plants and fruit. Later, some of them established semi-permanent farming villages. During the next 10,000 years, their people gradually spread all over the American continent.

As they migrated, they spread into regions with different climates and terrain. Some remained in the cold far north, while some spread into the woodlands of the northeast; others travelled further south, to the Great Plains and beyond. It is thought that about half a million of these first Americans lived in North America during the time covered by this book. Depending on where they lived, the people developed a way of life to suit their surroundings. Therefore the Plains culture was quite different from that of many other American peoples.

> **'Whose voice was first sounded on this land? The voice of the red people who had but bows and arrows.'**
>
> *—— Red Cloud of the Oglala Sioux ——*

THE GREAT PLAINS

The lands of the Plains Indians are called the Great Plains. They are a truly vast area which stretches from the Mississippi river in the east to the Rocky Mountains in the west and from Canada in the north to Texas in the south.

Today, this area is covered with wheat and corn, but until the 20th century this was grassland, or 'prairie' as it is known. The climate can be a blistering 35°C in summer, but can drop to a bitterly cold minus 20°C in winter.

Paintings and engravings by 'white' artists recorded how the Plains Indians appeared to early settlers and explorers. This colourful and dramatic portrait of Blackfoot chief Buffalo's Back Fat was painted by George Catlin in 1832.

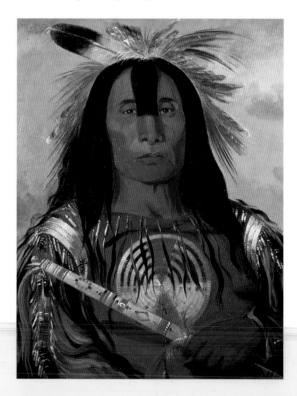

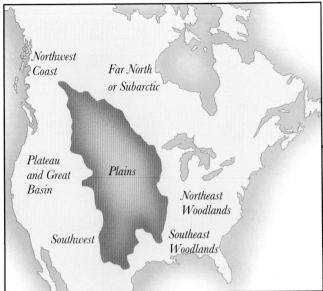

The area inhabited by the Plains Indians (shaded orange, left) covered an area about 2,000 km long and 1,200 km wide. Before thousands of white settlers transformed the Great Plains into wheatfields, huge herds of buffalo grazed on the prairie grasses of the region. Also shown are the areas of the six other main North American Indian cultures.

This map shows the homelands of the main Plains tribes in the 19th century. Many of these peoples were constantly moving and migrating. Each tribe had its own distinctive culture and language.

EXPLORERS FROM THE SEA

Life on the Plains was transformed by contact with the Europeans. Viking sailors are believed to have been the first to 'discover' North America. But the first real contact between Europeans and the native American peoples came after Christopher Columbus landed in 1492. Columbus had set sail on a voyage to search for a new way to the Indies (in the Far East), when, by chance, he discovered the Americas. He thought he had landed in the Indies, so called the people he met 'Indians'. Until the early 19th century, very few 'white men' visited the Great Plains.

The native Americans had no word to describe themselves as a whole nation. They were a people made up of hundreds of different tribes, each with their own culture and language. Many of them called themselves names which meant 'The People' or 'our people' in their own language. Most modern-day native Americans call themselves 'Native Americans' or 'First Americans', but Columbus' original term 'Indians' is still commonly used.

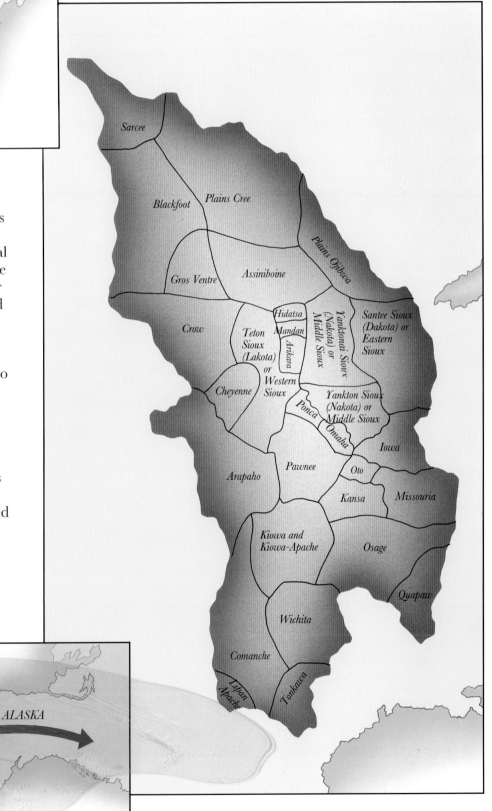

The land bridge between Asia and America. This route disappeared when the Ice Age ended and the sea level rose.

A Blackfoot Buffalo Women's Society, or Mototik Society, holds a solemn ceremony within a ring of the horse-drawn 'sledges' known as travois. Special societies were as important to the Blackfoot as they were to most of the other Plains tribes.

Plains Indian society was made up of many different tribes, or nations, each of which had its own language and way of life. The tribes traded with each other in times of peace, but fought each other when disputes over territory or some other kind of disagreement could not be settled peacefully.

TRIBES AND BANDS

A tribe was made up of smaller groups called bands. A band might consist of about 20 families who were often related, and who travelled, worked and fought together. Each band was usually led by a chief who was chosen by the people for his qualities of wisdom, generosity, strength and bravery.

The chiefdom was not like a hereditary royal family, and chiefships did not pass automatically from father to son, unless the son had distinguished himself. A chief did not always stay a chief until his death. Some were forced to retire through old age, or through a serious loss of wealth which made it impossible for them to perform important duties like giving feasts or providing for the poor.

CAMPS

Throughout the year, nomadic bands moved frequently from one campsite to another following the herds of buffalo. However, in the summer many bands would join together to make a large camp for the communal buffalo hunts or to perform the ritual of the Sun Dance.

FAMILIES AND CLANS

As well as being members of a tribe or nation, and a band, Indians also had strong family ties. The idea of the 'nuclear' family - parents and their own children as a separate family unit - was unknown to them. Instead, their family included other relatives. It was common for these family groups to include relatives of one parent only, in which case they were known as clans. Elderly mothers or fathers - 'matriarchs' or 'patriarchs' - were recognized as the heads of the clan and were treated with great respect.

Clan loyalties were very important. While a person could move from one band to another, clan membership was fixed.

SOCIETIES

As well as these ties, most men and women were members of special ritual organizations, or societies. Some, like the Crow Tobacco Society, were religious; others, like the Dog Soldiers, were warrior societies. Members of these societies often had special duties. The Dog Soldiers were a sort of military police whose role was to keep order inside the camp and on communal buffalo hunts; they also arranged raiding and hunting parties. Like most of the societies, the Dog Soldiers had magnificent costumes and masks which they used in elaborate dances and ceremonies.

This Hidatsa warrior is taking part in the Dog Dance, performed by members of the Dog Society. Many tribes had male societies with special officers, functions, costumes and songs. Men were graded by age and would advance from one society to another.

THE LAW

Each band was governed by its chief and his council - experienced warriors and other important members of the tribe, such as the *wicasa wakan* or 'man of mystery' (see pages 28-29). Wrong-doers were made to feel ashamed or ignored. In extreme cases, such as murder, the guilty person was exiled from the band - and a lone wanderer on the Plains rarely survived.

Tribal chiefs, like this Pawnee leader, ruled their people with the help and advice of respected and experienced members of the tribe, such as the 'man of mystery'. Each band's council was consulted on things that affected everyone, such as matters governing the camp, the hunt and warfare. The council made decisions based on the unanimous agreement of its members. They could not force anyone to do anything against their will, and they would give advice rather than orders.

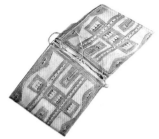

Parfleches - large storage containers made from buffalo or elk hide - were used to store dried buffalo meat and other foods. They were especially useful when people were on the move, travelling or hunting.

Draped with a wolfskin, hunters creep up on their quarry until they are close enough to shoot. The hunters must approach carefully or the cautious buffalo will smell them and be frightened away.

The buffalo was the most important animal on the Plains. Its meat provided nourishing food and its skin was made into clothing and tipi coverings. The Indians lived in harmony with this animal, killing only what they needed and using as much of each carcass as possible.

THE BUFFALO

The American buffalo, or bison, is a large, lumbering animal. The bulls can weigh more than a ton. The female cows are smaller but more valuable because they give better meat. Buffalos have a good sense of smell, but their eyesight is poor. If they feel threatened they can become very bad-tempered and will charge their enemy. Hunting them was therefore exhausting and dangerous.

Before the white man arrived there were about 50 million buffalo on the Plains. By 1900, only about 550 animals were left.

'The buffalo is our brother, almost part of ourselves. There is power in a buffalo, but there is no power in an Angus or a Hereford, man-bred animals.'

—— *Lame Deer, Sioux* wicasa wakan ——

THE HUNT

Large hunts took place in the summer, and everyone took part. The hunt involved special religious ceremonies. The band offered prayers and songs imploring the 'Great Mystery', Wakan Tanka (see page 28), to grant the hunters success in providing food and clothing for the band.

Scouts were sent out to find the herds. When they returned with news of their prey, a hunting party under the leadership of the chiefs would be organized. The band's Dog Soldiers acted as police to ensure that the hunt 'rules' were followed. It was an offence to hunt on one's own and frighten the herd.

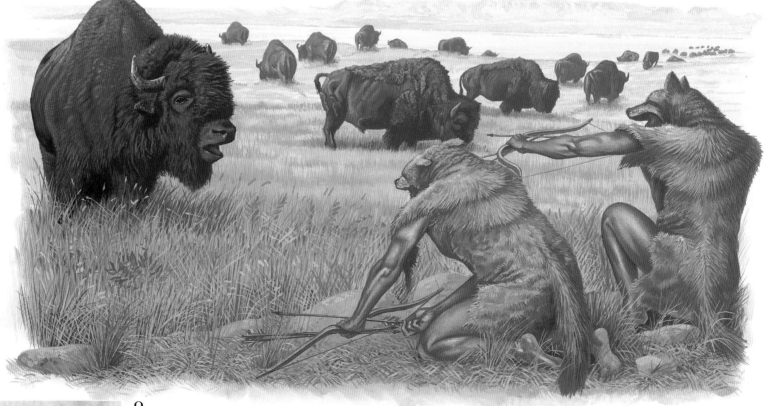

STEALTHY HUNTING

The earliest method of hunting was on foot. Disguised as wolves, with skins thrown over their bodies, the warriors would creep towards the herd, singing special songs to put a 'spell' on the animals. The buffalo did not usually run away from wolves, so they felt quite safe. The warriors were able to get close enough to kill their prey with arrows.

Another method involved forcing the buffalo through narrow canyons where the panic-stricken animals would become trapped, or they would be herded over cliffs and fall to their deaths.

AFTER THE HUNT

Although the whole tribe would share the kill, the best parts of the buffalo were given to those hunters who had made kills. Each hunter's arrows were specially marked, so they could easily identify which buffalo they had killed. The animals were skinned and cut up on the spot, and the meat and hides were then carried home. Hunting parties often had to travel long distances back to camp.

Once the hunting party had returned home, some of the meat was roasted or stewed, then feasted on by the whole band in celebration.

PEMMICAN AND JERKY

Meat that was not eaten fresh was cut into thin strips and hung up to dry. Then it could be ground up with fat and berries to make a food called pemmican. Strips of sun-dried meat that were not mixed with anything else were called jerky. Jerky didn't need to be cooked, although it was sometimes boiled before it was eaten. Pemmican could be stored for months without going off.

Hunting methods changed drastically with the arrival of the horse. Warriors on horseback would charge the herd, forcing a stampede. The confused animals could then be shot with arrows or stabbed with spears.

Huge amounts of buffalo meat were made into pemmican for use during the winter months when hunting was difficult.

THE ARRIVAL OF THE HORSE

Beadwork bags like this one were called tipi bags. They were used as general storage containers. They could also be used by hunters and warriors as saddlebags to carry their rations and ammunition. The Indians decorated their riding gear with great care.

The arrival of the horse on the Plains radically altered the lives of the native Americans. Hunting methods, travel, the siting of camps, tribal territory and many other aspects of life were never to be the same again. Many tribes that had lived in permanent villages for part of the year, took up their tipis and became travellers.

HORSES FROM SPAIN

The horse was first introduced into the area in the 1600s by the Spanish. At first, they tried to prevent the native peoples from getting horses, but their efforts were in vain. As the Plains Indians came to understand the horse's usefulness, animals began to disappear from Spanish villages. The Indians soon taught themselves to ride and manage these 'mysterious dogs', as they called them. As time went on, more horses came into the Indians' possession. They were often caught from the herds of ponies, or 'mustangs', that had escaped from white settlers and were roaming wild on the Plains.

HORSE CARE

The Indians valued and admired their horses. The task of caring for them was given to boys and young men. In the spring and summer, the horses were put out to pasture on the prairie. In winter, they were brought closer to the camp - sometimes they were tethered to tipi pegs or brought right inside earth lodges. At this time of year, their fodder consisted of cottonwood bark and branches.

HORSEMANSHIP

Great pride was taken in horsemanship, and the Plains Indians became some of the finest riders in the world. Special techniques were developed for hunting on horseback. Hunters and warriors became skilled at riding very fast in pursuit of their prey, whilst accurately aiming a spear or gun to make a kill.

Horse races were a particularly popular pastime, and they were highly competitive! There were no official race courses - the contests were usually wild gallops, with each rider whooping and shouting as he forced his animal on. Often, the winner of the race was awarded an eagle feather to wear in his hair.

OWNING HORSES

Once horses came to the Plains, more tribes, including the Cheyenne and Crow, decided to live as nomads looking for horses. People who had previously been isolated came into conflict with each other. Horses grew to be so valuable that wealth began to be measured by the number of

With its breathtaking speed and wild recklessness, an Indian horse race was always a popular spectacle. It was often difficult to tell whether the race was a purely sporting challenge or a serious battle for dominance amongst warriors.

Horse-stealing expeditions usually took place at night. Just before dawn, the warriors would leave a nearby hideout and ride stealthily towards the enemy's village where the horses were tethered. Often, as dawn broke, the warriors would charge headlong into the grazing herd, cutting them free and leading them away.

animals owned. This led to horse-stealing raids against other tribes. It was considered a great act of bravery to creep undiscovered into an enemy camp and take a horse without getting caught.

WEALTH AND PRESTIGE

Horses were even used as a kind of currency within the camp. The *wicasa wakan* might be paid in horses for a successful cure, for example, or horses might form part of a woman's dowry. A chief could gain considerable prestige by showing his generosity in making the gift of a horse to a poor member of his band.

Traditionally, the favourite horse of a man that had died would be killed and laid alongside his owner. Any other horse he had owned would be given away.

Catching wild horses was no easy feat. Riders would gallop towards the herd, each aiming to trap an escaping horse by throwing a lasso around its neck. Once caught, a terrified animal would often drag its captor along until it dropped down exhausted. The rider would then allow the animal to get its breath back and stand up. Taming, breaking in and training was merely a matter of time after that.

FARMING AND HUNTING

Indian women used heavy hammers like this to pound chokecherries against flat stone slabs. The pulp was then used to make pemmican. The hammers were used for other purposes, too - they were ideal for knocking in tipi pegs.

The main source of food for most Plains Indians was the mighty buffalo. They supplemented their diet with many kinds of wild fruit, including berries. They also hunted wild antelope for their meat, beavers for their fur, and eagles for their feathers.

Most of the farming was done by women, on plots of ground that were usually several kilometres from the village. To protect the growing crops, the women would build platforms from which they and their children could scare away birds.

FARMING

Some tribes, such as the Mandan and the Hidatsa, lived most of the time in villages of earth lodges (see page 16). They farmed the land, growing maize, beans, squash, pumpkins and sunflowers. Some of the crops were traded for animal skins and, later, for blankets and beads from the white man.

Famine and starvation were real threats for all the tribes. The herds of buffalo moved in unpredictable ways across the Plains. If the rain failed, the farmers and villagers might lose their crops in droughts. So, whenever possible, food was carefully stored for use in times of need.

MAIZE

Maize was the most important crop. There were two harvests, one in late summer, another in the autumn. At the summer harvest, part of the green corn was gathered, boiled or roasted, shelled, then dried and stored in bags. On the Upper Missouri river, sugar corn was left to ripen and then made into cornballs. Some tribes also harvested wild rice.

In the autumn, the rest of the maize was harvested. After separating the grains from the husks and stalk, the corn grains were stored in jug-shaped pits. These 'cache pits' could be over two metres deep and were lined with dried grass. Sometimes they were used to store vegetables, too.

GATHERING FOOD

It was the task of the women to tend the crops and gather food, usually helped by their older children. They picked fruits, such as wild strawberries, chokecherries and wild plums. Many of the fruits were dried in the sun and saved for the cold winter months. Herbs such as peppermint were picked and dried in the same way then mixed with ground-up meat to keep it fresh. Fish were not a common source of food, but tribes like the Blackfoot and the Omaha sometimes caught and ate them.

Tobacco was planted, picked and dried by tribes like the Hidatsa. In this case it was the old men rather than the women who tended the crop. Tobacco was primarily kept for ceremonies and other solemn occasions, and its use was often subject to rules and restrictions.

MEALS

The women also gathered wood for their cooking fires. Fresh meat was roasted on sticks or stewed with wild vegetables such as turnips. A favourite soup was made by boiling ribs and joints full of marrow. The Plains Indians used salt with their food, which they got from salt beds or salt springs, and later from white traders.

HOSPITALITY

The Plains Indians were generous people. They shared with those who were in need, remembering that the time might come when they might be hungry themselves. Most households kept a pot of stew cooking over a fire all day long. Visitors were always invited to share meals. Guests were honoured by being seated separately and served with the tastiest morsels. The families would not eat until the visitors had finished. At family meals the men ate first, the women later.

While the buffalo were hunted, other creatures such as owls, hawks, foxes, deer, porcupines and ermine were usually trapped. Hunters hid in pits covered with twigs, leaves and grass, leaving a peephole to spy through. They then placed an animal decoy at the edge to lure hungry birds and animals towards the trap. The hunter would spear his prey or grab it with his bare hands.

13

THE FAMILY

The umbilical cord of a newborn Sioux baby was traditionally placed in a pouch like this, specially made by the grandparents. The pouches were usually shaped like lizards, snakes or turtles, since these animals were respected for their long life and endurance and were believed to bring good luck and give protection. The pouches were fastened to the cradleboard or worn around the neck.

The family was important to everybody. Men and women carried out different but equally important tasks. The elderly, and children, were all highly valued members of the tribe.

THE DIVISION OF LABOUR

By tradition, it was the man who fought, hunted and went on raids. He also went out with scouting parties who searched out the buffalo herds and tracked enemies. One male tribe member was appointed to record the Winter Count (see page 19) - a kind of calendar or journal of memorable events.

The woman's role was primarily domestic, gathering or growing food. However, all the belongings of each family were the property of the women, apart from the men's weapons and hunting gear. And it was not unknown for a woman to break with tradition and fight and hunt alongside the men.

FAMILIES

Indians lived in extended families, where responsibility for the children was shared. This sometimes led to children calling their aunts and uncles 'father' and 'mother', too. This was a very practical arrangement. If a parent was lost through divorce or death, a child might still have several mothers or fathers to take care of it.

Most women got married between the ages of 12 and 14. Some couples married for love, but, more often, marriages were arranged by the tribe's elders. Sometimes men took more than one wife; a man might marry sisters, for example. Relations belonging to the same clan might also marry, although there were strict rules regulating who could marry who.

Marriages were sealed with an exchange of gifts between the two families. A new husband was expected to give horses, buffalo hides or blankets to his bride's father. Sometimes, men took more than one wife.

CHILDHOOD

The birth of a child was a happy event. The newborn baby was greased with buffalo fat and strapped into a cradle-board, a wooden frame with laces. The board was a symbol of protection for the new child, as well as a practical carrying device. It was often decorated lavishly with porcupine quills or beads.

NAMES

Soon after the birth, there would be a feast and a *wicasa wakan* would be asked to name the infant. Names were not always fixed for life. If a child got sick, it might get a new name once it had recovered. A boy returning from his first war party could be renamed, in recognition of his new-found manhood. His name could change again if he distinguished himself as a warrior.

EDUCATION

Children were taught the beliefs and values of the tribe by the elders. They were taught to respect the earth, and to understand the importance of becoming strong and useful members of society.

Naughty children were rarely punished by whipping or beating. Boys were disciplined by denying them the right to play at hunting, tracking or wargames. Girls had their dolls taken away. Crying was not tolerated - even a tiny baby's nose might be pinched to stifle its cries, in case the sound alerted an enemy close by.

PREPARATION FOR ADULTHOOD

Children everywhere learnt skills by imitating the adults in play. Indian boys looked after the horses and trained as warriors and hunters. By the time a boy was about 10 years old, his father would take him on short hunting trips. His first buffalo kill was an important event, marked by a communal feast and the giving of presents. Boys would ride out on their first war party when they were aged 13 or 14.

Young girls played with miniature tipis, cradleboards, dolls and replicas of household items. A girl's first menstruation marked her entry into womanhood and was celebrated with special rituals. Often she was separated from the rest of the tribe and instructed in her adult duties by a *wicasa wakan*, who fastened an eagle feather in her hair. She would also have a feast held in her honour.

A Kiowa mother with her baby in a cradleboard. Wrapped up snugly and strapped to the board, the baby could be kept out of harm's way, carried on its mother's back or suspended from the horse's saddle when moving camp.

All female relatives shared in the raising of the child. The sisters of the mother and father helped out with the practical care of their nephew or niece. Older women of the family, such as the grandmothers, would play their part later on by telling the child stories and teaching him or her important tribal customs.

A MANDAN VILLAGE

The see-through scene below shows two Mandan earth lodges. Several tribes, such as the Mandan, Omaha, Hidatsa and Pawnee, built lodges. The earth lodge was usually constructed around a large circular pit, about 30 cm deep and up to 30 metres wide. The frame was supported by 12 foundation posts. The height of the finished lodge was anything up to 18 metres. The walls and roof were covered with layers of prairie grass, willow branches and earth. A large smoke hole was left at the top, and there was an entrance at the side.

The Mandan were a Plains tribe which farmed the land and built permanent villages. They lived in earth homes called lodges, and used tipis (see page 30) only when they moved around. The Mandan villages were based around the Missouri river. Most were built on high ground, with the lodges arranged in a circle. The circle had a special meaning - it represented the earth. A village might have up to 100 lodges, including the chief's lodge and a 'medicine' lodge for important ceremonies.

THE VILLAGES

A Mandan village was usually surrounded by a strong stockade for protection. The lodges were set around a central shrine or sacred place. This was often the scene of colourful ceremonies and dances by the various societies of the village.

1   Lodge post
2   Shallow pit
3   Walls made of layers of prairie grass, willow and earth
4   Smoke hole

THE LODGE

The lodge was a domed construction, entered through a covered passage. Each part of the building was symbolically important - the entrance faced east towards the sunrise; and the roof represented the sky.

Between some of the lodges were storage pits and racks for drying the crops grown in fields outside the village. The platforms were built high up, safely away from animals, and could only be reached by climbing a ladder.

5　**Bed with hide curtains**
6　**Shields and weapons**
7　**Hearth**
8　**Chief's horses**
9　**Entrance to lodge**

STRONG AND STURDY

An earth lodge was a sturdy building. It might last for up to 10 years. The roofs could easily withstand the weight of several people - children often scampered across them, while the elders would traditionally stand on top of their homes to welcome the morning sun. A typical lodge could comfortably accommodate 30-40 people. Horses, too, could be squeezed inside in the winter. There were no windows: the only light that came in was through the smokehole or the entranceway.

Around the walls of most lodges were box-like beds with hide curtains. Seating was provided by carefully arranged skins and robes, with willow backrests for leaning against. A lodge would also be full of everyday items, such as cooking utensils, clothing and tools.

In this scene of part of a Mandan village, there are many people on the lodge roofs. Can you see the round boats that the Mandan used on the rivers? When you turn the see-through page, you can see inside the lodge of a Mandan chief. The scene is based partly on the journal of George Catlin, paintings by Karl Bodmer, and descriptions of lodges built by other tribes such as the Omaha and Hidatsa.

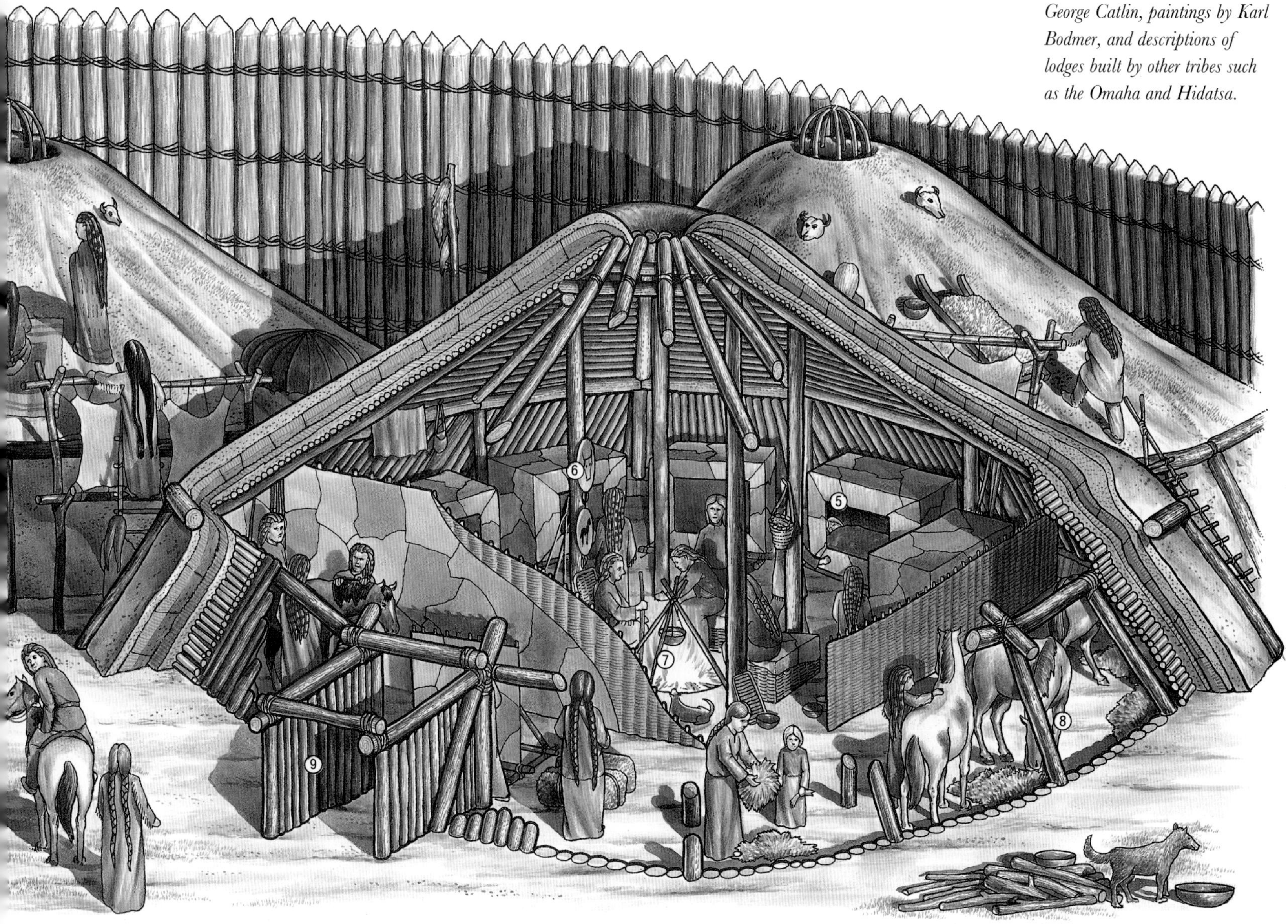

ART AND CRAFT

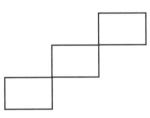

twisted

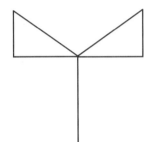

forked tree

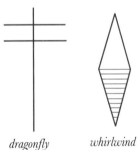

dragonfly   *whirlwind*

Colours and designs could have symbolic meanings. Amongst the Lakota, for example, red might mean the sunset or thunder, yellow the dawn clouds or earth, and blue the sky. Triangles stood for tipis, straight lines represented arrows. Certain designs belonged to particular families and were handed down from mother to daughter.

Art and craft were closely connected with the customs, religion and daily life of the Plains Indians. They considered that artistic expression was as necessary to their spiritual well-being as hunting the buffalo was to their physical survival.

PORTABLE ART

Much of the art of the wandering tribes was small - pieces that could be worn, rolled up and carried off to a new camp at a moment's notice. These included carved pipes, painted rawhide, and quillwork and beadwork on soft hides. Pottery and basketry were uncommon, since these items would have been heavy, breakable and bulky to carry. Instead, most containers were made from treated skins and were often lavishly decorated.

MATERIALS

Artists and craftspeople used materials they could find easily around them - skins, bones, hair, stone and materials from plants. The skin of the buffalo was not just a practical material for clothing and shelter. It was believed to contain the spirit of the animal from which it came, so beautifying a skin was a way of giving thanks and honour to that spirit.

QUILLS

Traditionally, women did all the quillwork and beadwork. Before the arrival of the white man, most embroidery made use of dyed porcupine quills, each one up to 10 centimetres long. Clothing, saddles and cradleboards were decorated with beautiful designs using these quills. The designs often had a symbolic meaning.

BEADS

Until European cloth became available, Indian women used black, red, yellow and blue vegetable dyes. Then, traders brought other materials that the women could use in their handiwork - metal buttons, ribbons and beads. By the 19th century, the Indians were trading eagerly for beads of coloured Venetian glass called 'pony beads'. Later on, smaller 'seed beads' from Venice and Czechoslovakia replaced the pony beads. Seed beads were available in greater quantities, and this meant larger areas could be decorated.

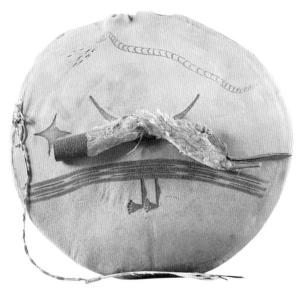

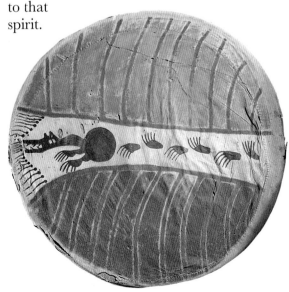

Painted designs on tipis, or on dance and war shields, had a strong significance for their owners. The shield on the left shows a bear coming out of a hole; that above features a snake and buffalo. These motifs could be used to give their owners divine protection, or they could be the symbols of a special society.

TRIBAL PATTERNS

Each tribe had its own designs and colour combinations. These patterns were usually basic shapes combined in a variety of ways. The Crow liked large triangles, rectangles, diamonds and hourglasses in blue, green, yellow and pink; the Sioux preferred triangles, crosses and rectangles in white, red, blue, yellow and green.

PAINTING

Men were usually responsible for painting robes, tipi covers and the 'Winter Counts', a sort of pictorial tribal history which included descriptions of battles, exploits and personal visions. These paintings were more life-like and usually featured motifs such as horses, birds, animals and people.

These Blackfoot leggings and Sioux moccasins are decorated with intricate beadwork and quillwork.

PIPES

Men and women smoked pipes for pleasure as well as ceremony (see page 29). All pipes were believed to contain spiritual power and so were treated with reverence. Personal pipes were plain, but those used in ceremonies were elaborately decorated.

Pipe stems were decorated with plaited porcupine quills, feathers and carving. The feathered pipes were known as calumets. They were sometimes carved in the shape of an animal or human, and many of the designs depicted myths and stories. In some calumets, feathers were grouped together so that when the pipe was shaken during a dance, it looked like a flying bird.

Painting the Winter Count, a sort of historical calendar marking the time between the first snowfall of one year and the next. The pictures on the buffalo hide show important happenings such as battles, spiritual events, and disasters.

Pipe bowls, like this one in the shape of a seated woman, were carved from catlinite, a red stone mined from a quarry in Minnesota. It was believed that Wakan Tanka himself had carved himself a pipe from this quarry. One story says that the stone there was made from the petrified blood of the Indians' ancestors and buffalo.

19

This is a bone awl, used for working tough rawhide. Implements used for preparing skins were sometimes made from buffalo horns or deer antlers.

Plains Indians wore ceremonial clothing some of the time, but their everyday clothing was much simpler. The women wore loose dresses, and the men wore breechcloths (a long piece of soft tanned deerskin that hung from a belt), shirts and leggings. Both men and women wore buffalo robes on top of their other clothes, and moccasins on their feet.

PREPARING HIDES

Originally, all these clothes were made from animal skins, but when trading with the white man began, blankets and cloth obtained from the traders were also used for garments.

The women were responsible for making clothing. They used the skins of buffalo, moose and deer. The hides were specially prepared to make them soft and supple, then sewn together using an awl (a sort of needle) and buffalo or deer sinew.

RAWHIDE

Rawhide was used for shields, parfleches and for the soles of footwear known as moccasins. It was produced by first scraping the fat and tissue off the hide with a scraper. Unless the skin was going to be made into a robe, all the hair was removed as well. The hide was then left to dry and bleach in the sun before being scraped again to achieve the same thickness all over.

SOFT LEATHER

To make softer leather, the scraped rawhide was rubbed with a mixture of buffalo grease and brains, and softened in warm water. It was then rolled up and left for a few days to 'season'. At this point it would shrink and had to be stretched back to its original size on a purpose-built frame. Finally, the stretched hide was washed and scraped with sandstone until it was soft, supple and dry. This whole process, which we call tanning, produced a beautifully soft leather that could be worked easily.

Tanning and stretching buffalo hides was a common chore for the women. The leather produced in this way was usually a pale beige or pinkish colour. Some skins were smoked by hanging them over smouldering fires to give them a darker brown colour.

DRESSES

One of the most common styles of women's dress was made from two animal skins, sewn together at the top with holes for the head and arms. The women's dresses were usually fringed and decorated with beautiful beaded designs. Dresses were sometimes worn with decorated rawhide belts, and tight-fitting leggings were usually worn underneath.

There were many styles of dress on the Plains. Here are just a few examples of what was worn.

ROBES

For extra warmth, buffalo robes were worn over the shoulders and wrapped around the body. They were painted with geometric designs, pictorial representations of battles and other memorable events. Some were elaborately quilled or beaded. A spectacular design could identify a chief, or other important person.

Blankets introduced by the traders were often used instead of robes. This was probably because the wool was lighter, less bulky, and didn't require the intensive preparation of a buffalo hide.

Chief Mato-tope, an important Mandan warrior, posed in ceremonial dress for painter Karl Bodmer. He wears an impressive feather headdress, a painted buffalo robe and embroidered moccasins.

MOCCASINS

Moccasins were made from soft skin, with rawhide soles. They were sewn together with thread made from sinew. It was common for women to re-use their discarded tipi covers for clothing, and moccasins were sometimes made out of the old tipi smoke flaps which had been made 'waterproof' from the smoke.

Breechcloths and moccasins were the men's chosen clothing in the hot summer months. This warrior is also wearing a ceremonial warbonnet of eagle tail feathers.

A Comanche wearing a European-style army hat. Frequent contact between Indians and whites led to the adoption of 'untraditional' items of clothing.

Dakota Sioux women wore robes like this to keep warm in cold weather.

In the cold winter, Blackfoot men wore coats made from blankets, fur hats, mittens and moccasins stuffed with grass.

DECORATION

T he Plains people wore many ornaments. These included necklaces, feathers and other hair ornaments, silver and bead earrings, armbands, wristbands and anklets for both personal decoration and religious ceremony. They also wore bead chokers and simple strings of beads or animal claws, and decorated bone breastplates.

Grizzly bear claws were believed to hold great spiritual power by most Indian tribes, and were often made into highly-prized necklaces for ceremonial use.

ORNAMENTS

Many Plains Indians had their ears pierced at an early age, sometimes as part of a ceremony. Each ear generally had a single hole, although some tribes, such as the Comanche, preferred several holes and wore a small earring in each. Earrings were made of silver wires strung with shell, silver and glass beads.

Armbands and anklets were usually part of dance outfits, and not worn every day. They were decorated with quills, beads and strips of fur, often with claws or hooves still attached.

BODY-PAINTING

People regularly painted their faces and hair with paints made from powdered earth, clay and rocks. These colours were usually reds, yellows and browns. Some painting was done according to dreams or visions. Thus the designs had a very personal meaning for the wearer.

'They paint their faces red with vermillion; this colour, which they procure by barter from the traders, is rubbed with fat, which gives them a shining appearance. Others colour only the edges of their eyelids, and some stripes in the face.'

Prince Maximilian

Warriors traditionally painted their faces and horses with bright designs before they went to war. This was to express their power and was meant to frighten their enemies. The designs might describe acts of bravery or success in battle, or show membership of a warrior society. Plains Indians also tattoed themselves. This was done partly for beauty, but more often as a result of a dream believed to be of great spiritual significance (see page 28).

22

HEADDRESSES

Both men and women decorated their heads with headdresses of buckskin, strips of fur, and even whole animal skins. Men's headdresses identified their status in a tribe, or membership of a society. A single feather usually represented a war deed.

Warbonnets and other elaborate headdresses were worn only for special occasions. They were made of quills, fur, feathers and buffalo horn and were often worn to show high status or courage and bravery in war. The wearing of a war-bonnet was not necessarily reserved for a chief.

Hairstyles and headdresses, of men in particular, were many and varied. Many Plains women, on the other hand, wore their long hair parted in the middle, with two braids.

Roach

Braids

Blackfoot with single feather

Assiniboine with horned headdress

A Crow warrior had to perform many acts of bravery before he was awarded the honour of wearing this feathered headdress or warbonnet. Each feather represented the brave deed of an individual warrior or tribe.

HAIR

Hair was often of symbolic importance, and some tribes believed that the hair was part of the soul. Style was generally chosen according to tribal tradition, or personal dreams and visions, as well as personal taste. The hair could be worn loose and long, perhaps with a painted parting; or carefully plaited or braided; or cut short or completely cropped. Hair style sometimes reflected a particular event in a person's life. Widows and mourners, for example, would traditionally cut their hair to show their grief.

For men, their hair was an especially valuable ornament. It might be knotted on top of their head, or greased so that it stood up in a huge point or curve. Some men would shave their heads, leaving only a single strip of hair on top. This strip, called a roach, might be made to stick upright with a stiff coloured fringe of feathers or animal hair.

'Cut an enemy's throat'

'Killed an enemy'

'Wearer wounded many times'

'Third coup'

'Fourth coup'

'Killed an enemy and took his scalp'

'Fifth coup'

Honour feathers were awarded for acts of bravery (called counting coup - see page 38). Feathers were coloured or cut to represent particular deeds.

THE SWEAT LODGE

The 'sweatbath' was one of the most ancient of American rituals. It took place in a special lodge, and was undertaken as an act of spiritual purification. People who danced the Sun Dance, for example, prepared themselves by taking a sweatbath first. Some tribes, such as the Comanche, used sweatbaths for medicinal purposes, believing that they cured complaints like rheumatism. And George Catlin recorded that the Mandan took sweatbaths as 'an everyday luxury by those who have time and energy or industry to indulge in it'.

According to George Catlin, the Mandans took sweatbaths for both spiritual and medicinal purposes (below). He described how the sweat lodge was placed near the river, with a small fire set into the bank. The bather sat in a 'crib or basket, much in the shape of a bathing-tub, curiously woven with willow boughs'. Then his wife would place a hot stone under him, and he or a helper would pour water over it to make 'a profusion of vapour'.

CONSTRUCTION

The sweat lodge was built from willow branches, bent to make a beehive-shaped frame. Buffalo hides or, later, fine-patterned blankets were placed over the top. The floor was covered with a herb called sage, for the bathers to sit on. In the centre of the lodge was a circular pit, representing the centre of the world. A small altar of stones, for the sacred pipe and tobacco offerings, was built inside the pit. On the altar, fragrant sweetgrass was burned to perfume the air.

The scooped-up earth from the circular pit was formed into a small, narrow ridge about three metres long, leading out of the lodge. The end of the ridge was marked by a mound called 'grandmother' - the name by which the earth was known.

HEATED STONES

Special stones were used in the ceremony. They were chosen for their dullness and hardness, so they would not explode when they got red hot. The stones were addressed as 'aged one' or 'grandfather', and were believed to contain great power. They were heated on a fire near the mound.

Up to eight persons could fit inside a typical sweat lodge, squatting on the floor. They took off their clothes before entering. First, red hot stones were brought from the fire by a helper and placed in the pit. The helper would then leave, closing the entrance flap to keep in the heat.

1 **Mandan sweat lodge**
2 **Crib over hot stones**
3 **Heated stones**
4 **Sioux *wicasa wakan***
5 **Helper**
6 **Ceremonial pipe**
7 **Heated stones**
8 **Sage spread on sweat lodge floor**

THE CEREMONY

A ceremonial pipe was passed around as various chants and prayers were said. Then, ice-cold water was poured onto the red hot stones. Clouds of steam filled the whole lodge. As the temperature rose people would begin to sweat. The heat was intense, until after a time the flap would be opened to let in cool air and light, and allow those inside to cool off.

A SYMBOLIC REBIRTH

This ritual was performed four times - four being a sacred number. At the end, the participants would run from the lodge and plunge into the cold water of a nearby stream to refresh themselves. This emergence into the outside world was seen as a symbolic rebirth, or purification of the body and mind.

In the scene below, a Sioux wicasa wakan is performing a sweatbath ceremony in preparation for the Sun Dance. The illustration is based on descriptions by Sioux ceremonial chiefs and wicasa wakans Fools Crow and Lame Deer. The picture above shows a fire pit, where sacred stones were heated before they were carried into the sweat lodge.

MUSIC AND DANCE

Music, dance and ceremony were used to celebrate and offer prayers to the spirits. There was hardly a task or an event that didn't have its own song or dance. There were also dances that belonged to men and women as well as different societies.

SINGING

Most of the music was sung, with a simple accompaniment on a drum. Songs were based on personal observation of the world around and sometimes included sounds from hunting and the wild.

DRUMS AND RATTLES

The singer was often accompanied by drums and rattles. There were two kinds of drum. The first was a hand drum rather like a modern tambourine, consisting of a single skin stretched across a small frame. The other type was made from a large hollowed-out section of tree trunk with strips of hide stretched across the top and bottom to act as the 'skins'. This drum was sometimes hung from forked sticks, and played with wooden drumsticks.

Rattles were made from gourds, turtle shells, moulded rawhide, and animal skins stretched over a wooden frame. These had pebbles or pieces of rawhide inside to make them rattle. The Dog Soldiers of the Hidatsa tribe traditionally used 'deerclaw' rattles, made from a stick with deer or antelope hooves attached. As well as providing accompaniment for singers, rattles were also used in various rituals. For example, a 'man of mystery' might shake a rattle over a sick person.

Decorated rattles were most often used to accompany the voice of either a singer or a healer. This one from the Blood (Blackfoot) tribe is made of moulded and sewn rawhide.

Many tribes performed a version of the Sun Dance, which always required lengthy preparations. The painted pole, around which the dancers moved, was made from a sacred tree, felled in a special ceremony conducted by a wicasa wakan.

OTHER INSTRUMENTS

The Indians also played instruments such as wooden flutes, often used by young lovers as a means of communicating. Messages like 'I'm here' or 'Meet me tomorrow' could be sent to one another in a sort of musical code. Another wind instrument was a kind of whistle, made from the wing bones of birds.

'DANCE GAZING AT THE SUN'

The most important dance of all was the yearly Sun Dance, performed at a festival that was celebrated all over the Plains. This ancient ceremony honoured the mysterious power of the sun which warmed the world after the cold winter. It was also an offering to Wakan Tanka, asking him to bring peace and prosperity.

Only men could take part in the Sun Dance. The dancers had usually vowed to take part in return for spiritual favours granted to them over the last year such as the healing of a sick relative, or for success in battle. The ceremony went on for four days. It took many days to prepare and four days for the performance itself. The dancers circled round a sacred tree symbolizing the sun, copying the way the sun moves in the sky. Some of them would go into a trance or have visions. Others, who had previously vowed to undergo tests of courage, were fastened to the pole with leather thongs which pulled at their skin as they moved, until they broke free.

THE GHOST DANCE

In the late 1880s, during the wars with the white man, a new dance was invented. A Paiute Indian called Wovoka dreamed that the Great Mystery told him that his people must prepare for the conquest of the white man. They were to dance the Ghost Dance, which would bring the Great Mystery down to Earth to resurrect the dead and bring back the buffalo. The dancers should wear special clothing with sacred designs to protect them from the white man's bullets.

'Then while Indians way up high, big flood comes like water and all white people die, get drowned... then nobody but Indians everywhere and game all kinds thick... Indians who don't dance, who don't believe in this word, will grow little, just about a foot high, and stay that way. '

— *Wovoka* —

The Ghost Dance spread like wildfire across the Plains, but it did not, in the end, save the tribes from destruction.

Wearing decorated masks, the warriors of the Mandan Bull Society jump, stomp and creep along the ground, imitating as closely as possible the movements of the buffalo. This was one of the most famous of the society dances, and was performed when buffalo were scarce and famine threatened.

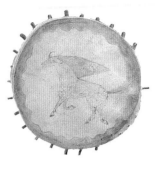

The beat of hand drums was a common feature of military society rituals in particular. The symbols used to decorate them often had a religious significance.

This sacred bundle from the Crow tribe contains the skin of a bird wrapped in cloth. Sacred bundles were sometimes opened and used in religious rituals and ceremonies.

Indian peoples believed it was important to live in harmony with their world, since the Earth provided them with everything they needed to survive. Indians never sought to control nature; instead they respected it and were thankful for the blessings it gave them.

THE 'GREAT MYSTERY'

The Plains Indians believed that everything on the Plains was imbued, or filled, with the spirit of the creator of the world, the 'Great Spirit' or 'Great Mystery'. To the Lakota Sioux, for example, he was known as Wakan Tanka. Wakan Tanka had arranged the world so that all living things could help each other, and he allowed the Plains Indians to live on the land.

They also believed that each creature had its own spirit or spiritual power, too. These spiritual powers helped people find food and shelter, protected them from injury and granted them success in battle.

SPIRITUAL CONNECTION

Because they believed everything has this spiritual power, everything in the Plains peoples' lives had a spiritual importance, too. For example, offending the spirits brought bad luck, so offerings were made and rituals performed to keep them happy. Some rituals, like the Sun Dance, involved the whole community; others, such as the vision quest, were personal experiences. And even ordinary, everyday tasks were accompanied by prayer.

WAKAN

The Plains Indians had one word for anything about the world they found mysterious or difficult to understand. For the Lakota Sioux that word was *wakan*. It was used to describe the earth and the heavens, the weather, and all aspects of nature. It was used in the names of objects connected with religious ritual, and in the sacred place names where ceremonies were held. It was also used for some of the unfamiliar things that arrived with the white man - the Sioux term for horse, *sunka wakan*, is literally 'mysterious dog', and for gun, *maza wakan*, means 'mysterious iron'!

VISIONS

Visions of guidance were much sought-after by the Plains Indians. They hoped to have them in their dreams or during personal journeys, or 'vision quests'. These quests were undertaken for many reasons. Sometimes, if bad luck struck, a person would journey to seek help from the spirits.

Vision quests were also undertaken at certain stages of a person's life. It was usual for a young man in his late teens to be sent to an isolated place to seek a personal vision. He would spend four days fasting, praying and calling on the spirits to aid him. If the quest was successful, the young man would be visited by a spirit who would talk to him and become his guardian. Afterwards, he could call on this guardian if he needed aid or protection.

A warrior's shield was one of his most important and sacred possessions. Before use, the shield was ceremonially made wakan *by painting and decorating it according to its owner's personal vision.*

28

A person's spirit guardian would probably appear in the form of an animal, a bird or a tree. The guardian would then teach certain songs and prayers which the vision seeker would use in his rituals. This picture, called 'Of the Owl's Telling', was painted in 1965 by Blackbear Bosin, a Kiowa-Comanche Indian.

The 'man of mystery' shown above is asking his guardian spirit, a bear spirit, for power to make an ill person well. For this reason he is wearing an entire skin of a grizzly bear. 'Men of mystery' are sometimes also known as holy or medicine men. The term medicine man is a 'white man's' term referring usually to a person who healed using spiritual means and herbal medicines.

'MEN OF MYSTERY'

Men who had very powerful visions often became holy men. Called *wicasa wakan*, or 'men of mystery', by the Sioux, they were believed to possess special powers, including the important ability to heal sick people. Every nation had its own term for this person. A *wicasa wakan* got his power from his guardian spirit, his prayers and his songs.

PIPES AND BUNDLES

Pipes were always used in religious ceremonies. The tobacco put in them was considered a sacred plant. It was believed that the rising smoke carried prayers up to the Wakan Tanka.

Some people, particularly *wicasa wakan*, carried special buffalo skin bags. These bags contained objects related to the person's visions - a mixture of plants, stones, weapons and feathers. This sacred and personal bundle of goods was believed to protect a person from illness and danger.

A NOMADIC LIFE

This painting by Karl Bodmer shows a Mandan 'dog-sledge'. In winter, some tribes travelled by toboggan. These were sledges without runners, made of wooden boards bent upward at the front and tied together with leather straps. Teams of dogs pulled them along, over the frozen rivers and streams.

The nomadic Plains tribes, like the Sioux or the Blackfoot, lived in cone-shaped homes called tipis. Tipis could be put up and taken down quickly so that the tribes could easily follow the herds of buffalo.

'When the chief decides that camp is to be moved, his herald goes through the village in the evening, crying out "Prepare, prepare! Tomorrow we move!" And again at the first blush of day he rides from end to end of the village, calling "Hunhunheeeeeee! Today the chief says we move toward the buffalo! Men, bring in the horses; women, throw down the lodges!" '

— *Edward Curtis* —

THE TRAVOIS

A travois was used to carry the tipi covers. It consisted of a frame made up of two long poles, which were tied with straps to the shoulders of a dog or a horse. The load was placed on a 'platform' or ladder-shaped frame fixed at the ends of the poles that trailed along the ground.

Before the coming of the horse, the Indians had only dogs to pull the travois, or had to carry their own packs. Therefore their tipis were relatively small. Sometimes a load was strapped directly to the dog's back, but a much heavier load could be pulled using the travois - as much as 30 kilograms if the animal was a strong one.

HORSE-DRAWN HOMES

Horses, of course, could pull even heavier loads, and travelled more quickly. A horse travois could also be used to carry small children, the elderly, or sick or wounded persons. For this, a dome-shaped structure of willow branches was attached to the poles to protect the person if the travois overturned. It must have looked a bit like a moving cage!

As many as five horses might be needed to carry a large tipi and all its furnishings, although three were usually enough. When a band needed to cross a deep river, the horses were unpacked. Simple 'rafts' were made using the lodge poles and pieces, and any available driftwood, and the band's goods were floated across.

BUILDING THE TIPI

The women put up the tipi. The frame was made of four pine or cedar poles that were hoisted up, then fastened near the top with rawhide cord. More poles were then leaned against them to form a cone. The hide cover was tied to the top of the last pole, lifted into place using the travois as a ladder, then wrapped around the 'cone' and joined together with lacing or pins. It took the effort of several women to lift the heavy cover. Sometimes one woman had to stand on the shoulders of another in order to reach the top.

Preparations for moving on would begin at dawn, when the women would take down the tipis and tie the poles to the horses' sides. Next, they would load the tipi covers and furnishings on to the travois. Parfleches of pemmican and jerky would then be hung on the saddles. On a signal from the chief, a long line would form and move slowly off.

SMOKE FLAPS AND STAKES

Once the cover was pinned together, two more poles were attached to the smoke flaps. These controlled the draught which carried away the smoke from the fire inside.

A long rawhide rope was left hanging from the poles and tied securely to a heavy stake driven into the ground inside. This helped stabilise the tipi and prevented it from being blown down in high winds. The tipi cover was usually fixed to the ground with wooden pegs, but in warm weather the bottom was rolled up to allow air to circulate.

Tipi covers were sewn together with thick buffalo sinew. Some covers were made of up to a dozen buffalo hides. When new, the hide was almost white, but with handling and use, and the smoke of the tipi fire, it gradually turned a rich brown and became softer and more flexible.

A stuffed bald eagle clutching a weasel skin in its talons. Items like this were tied to tipi poles and were believed to have special protective powers.

TIPIS

The see-through scene below shows some of the different types of tipi that might be found in a camp. Usually, the tipis would be more widely spaced and probably not arranged like this. The nomadic Plains tribes set their tipis in a circle, with the large council tipi in the centre. There would be one or more tipis where the tribe's societies met, and the 'man of mystery's' tipi, where he might perform rituals and healing. Also shown is a chief's tipi, and several belonging to the band's families. Traditionally, each family had its own place in the circle.

The site of each new tipi camp was usually decided some time before a move. Most tribes and bands had favourite camping places, close to water and good pasture for their horses. During the winter, bands would pitch their tipis in sheltered valleys or woods which offered them some protection from the cold. But in the summer, when all the tribe was together and the weather was warm, they camped on the open prairie in a great circle.

DECORATION

Tipis, also known as lodges, were strong and comfortable. They gave protection against the rain and hot sun, as well as the freezing cold. Some tribes, like the Sioux and the Blackfoot, often painted their tipis. Others, such as the Crow, rarely did.

Heavily painted tipis were very special and were usually owned by chiefs or 'men of mystery'. Warriors commonly decorated their tipis with designs representing their war exploits. Other designs might represent a personal vision.

INSIDE THE TIPI

The inside of a family's tipi was quite roomy and comfortable, although adults had to stoop to enter through the door flap. The doorway always faced east, towards the rising sun, and away from the prevailing west winds. On entering a tipi, a man was required to step to the right, a woman to the left. It was also good manners to walk behind a seated person, who would lean forward if necessary.

1 **Warrior society's large tipi**
2 **Smoke flap**
3 **Backrest**
4 **Man of mystery's tipi**
5 **Personal bundle**
6 **Family tipis**
7 **Chief's tipi**
8 **Large council tipi**
9 **Sacred altar**

FURNITURE

At the centre of the tipi was a small fire that burned virtually smokeless dried buffalo dung. Beside this was the family altar, where the smoke of sweetgrass and other incense perfumed the air. Beds were arranged around the edges, and were covered with buffalo robes. The family and guests sat on skins and robes, and leaned against backrests made from willow rods and sinew. The head of the family, or a special guest occupying the place of honour, sat at the back.

Food and clothing were stored along the sides in soft leather tipi bags, and in parfleches. Sacred bundles and war trophies were hung from the poles. In winter or during bad weather, food was prepared over the fire inside the tipi.

Some of the activities that might take place in a Plains Indian camp are shown in the scene below. Women are tanning buffalo hides and erecting a tipi. In the sparsely-furnished council lodge, a warrior is attending a sacred altar, while the man of mystery is seeking spiritual guidance in his heavily-painted tipi. Meanwhile, in the chief's tipi, his two wives are talking. Many chiefs provided a tipi for each of their wives.

DEATH AND BURIAL

A tree grave at a remote location, rather than a scaffold, was sometimes chosen as a final resting place.

The Plains peoples did not particularly fear death - they saw it more as a continuation of their present life. They believed that a person's soul would live on after death, and carried out ceremonies to prepare them for a journey into the next world.

THE AFTERLIFE

They believed that the soul travelled to the next world along a road suspended from heaven to earth known as the 'Hanging Road'. People lived in the next world just as they did in this one - hunting buffalo, playing games, and living in tipis. In heaven they were close to Wakan Tanka and their long-lost relatives and friends.

The Indians did not generally believe in a hell of any sort. They believed that all wrongdoing was punished on earth.

MOURNING

In spite of the happy afterlife that awaited the dead, those left behind mourned deeply. They made a great display of their grief by wailing and crying loudly, cutting their hair and even gashing their flesh. All of the dead person's property was given away. The dead person's tipi would be either abandoned or exchanged for another one.

This scene showing a burial scaffold is based on a painting by Karl Bodmer. The dead of the Sioux and Cheyenne were placed at the top of scaffolds of poles or saplings, so that animals could not reach the bodies. Other tribes erected a special funeral tipi, whereas the Arapaho buried their dead in the ground.

CEREMONIES

A dead person's body was looked after by his or her relatives. First, the hair was combed, the body was dressed in fine clothes and the face was painted red. An elaborate ceremony - the Ghost Keeper ceremony - then took place to honour the person. During this, a lock of hair was cut off and kept. The body was then laid on soft buffalo robe and wrapped tightly in skins that were tied securely with thongs.

The mourning period lasted four days. On the last night there was a feast, with ceremonial pipe smoking and offerings of food to the spirits. The lock of hair taken from the corpse was put into a sacred bundle with the hair of other deceased family members. These bundles were very precious and looked after by the women.

Mandan women tending their dead. They visited the rings of skulls daily, replacing any dried-up sage with fresh sage, and making offerings of food.

VILLAGES OF THE DEAD

Few tribes buried their dead under the ground. Instead, they erected a high scaffold of four posts. The body was put to rest on the scaffold, with its feet facing the rising sun. The scaffolds were high to keep away the wolves and other wild animals which roamed about.

Some bodies were laid in tree graves, similar to the scaffolds but supported by trees instead of posts. Occasionally, painted burial tipis were used for the bodies of chiefs or *wicasa wakan*. When an important person like this died, a scarlet or blue cloth was laid over the body as a mark of respect.

BURIAL GOODS

A filled pipe, food and the dead person's possessions were placed alongside the body. A warrior might be laid to rest with his feather-decked coup stick (see page 38), painted shield, and even the body of his favourite horse, killed so that its spirit might accompany its owner's into the afterlife. A woman might be surrounded with her household utensils.

CEMETERIES OF SKULLS

In time, the burial scaffolds decayed and the bones of the dead person dried and became bleached and purified. The bones would then be buried in caves or crevices in the rocks. The Mandan placed the skulls on sage circles. Medicine poles were placed in the middle of the circles to guard and protect the holy place. People visited their dead friends and relatives, to take them offerings of food and to talk with their spirits.

STORYTELLING

Storytelling was a popular and important activity, particularly during winter when the evenings were long and cold. They were often told by a storyteller, a special person who was looked on as an artist, a creator and a 'man of mystery'.

A favourite character in Plains Trickster myths is Coyote. Old Man Coyote is greedy and sly. He is always up to mischief. In many tales, he is an adversary to overcome, perhaps through trials of strength or battles of wit and cunning. Trickster myths are often funny, told to make the audience laugh out loud.

LEARNING A LESSON
The stories were meant to teach as well as entertain. A character might well be introduced to teach children important lessons on how to trap the buffalo, or how to perform a victory dance to give thanks to the spirits.

Some stories were told through colourful paintings on clothing and tipi covers, or elaborate carvings on sacred pipes. They were never written down, since the Indians did not have a system of writing like ours. Sometimes important myths were also danced or sung.

CREATION MYTHS
There are several types of myth. Creation myths, for example, explain how the world and its inhabitants were first created. They tell of a time when people ate their food raw, because they had no knowledge of fire, and when death was unknown to the people of the Plains.

Some creation myths go on to tell what happened to change the world, and how the present state of the world came about.

HERO AND SACRED MYTHS
Hero myths tell of the exploits of a hero. In one hero myth of the Crow tribe, an Indian woman gives birth to a child whose father is the sun. The child is gifted with power over wild animals, and tames a fierce bear and other dangerous creatures. At the end of the story he ascends into the sky and turns into a star.

Sacred myths usually explain the origin of a religious ritual. For example, the rules for ceremonial pipe-smoking were derived from the myth of Buffalo Calf Woman. Long ago, two scouts were hunting buffalo when they saw a beautiful woman coming towards them. One scout's mind was filled with bad thoughts and he was immediately turned into a skeleton. The other recognised the woman as a holy being. She told him to return to his tribe and build a tipi ready for her to visit. This he did. When the woman again appeared, she presented the chief of the tribe with the Sacred Pipe, explaining how to use it. She then walked out of the tipi, and changed miraculously from a woman into a white buffalo. The creature then disappeared from sight.

13 MOONS ON TURTLE'S BACK

Mythical beliefs were also behind the calendar that the Plains peoples used. They divided up the year using the cycles of day and night and the phases of the moon. Because the moon waxed and waned over 28 days, this meant that a year was made up of 13 lunar cycles rather than the 12 months of the year that we use.

THE MOONS

Many tribes named each moon of the year after a natural event associated with that time of year. For example, the 'Moon of Falling Leaves' would be in the autumn. Each moon was also believed to have a story attached to it. This story was given power by the Turtle, who held the mystery of each moon in its shell. The same moon might have more than one name, because so many different things could happen at that time.

Stories were told on winter evenings, when the people had stretched out to relax at the end of the day. A narrator might talk on and on into the night, stopping only when lack of response suggested that most of his audience had fallen asleep, lulled by his words and the warmth of the camp fire.

The yearly cycle, as observed by the Plains people, is described in the Turtle myth. The 13 large scales on its shell stand for the 13 moons in any one year. For many tribes, most moons had a name, according to the season, for example:
Moon of the Popping Trees;
Moon of the Dark Red Calf;
Moon of the Snowblind;
Moon of the Grass;
Moon When the Ponies Shed;
Moon of Making Fat;
Moon When the Calf Grows Hair;
Moon When the Wolves Run Together.

Symbols from myths and stories were often beaded onto clothing. The thick blue area on this Sioux dress is symbolic of Takuskanskan ('sky'). The thinner blue line below represents a lake or body of water where Turtle dwells.

37

WARFARE

These warriors, from rival war parties, are 'counting coup'. A 'coup' could be won by striking the body of an enemy (either dead or alive), by capturing a horse, or by taking a scalp. While killing an enemy might be good for a warrior's reputation, it was not usually necessary for him to do so. In fact, there was no disgrace in running away, so a warrior who fought to the death might be considered stupid.

Warfare was commonplace in the lives of the Plains peoples. Some tribes were enemies with other tribes, and conflict between them could last for years. For example, the Cheyenne and the Mandan were bitter foes. However, the tribes did not try to steal land from each other, or conquer one another - they fought to defend their hunting lands, capture horses, show their strength and prove their bravery as warriors. Successful warriors would boast of their deeds at a victory dance, especially if they had taken the scalps of their enemies.

LEARNING TO FIGHT

All the Plains Indians admired strength and courage and a man was expected to be brave. From childhood, boys were trained to be warriors - men who were able to endure hunger, thirst, discomfort and danger. A warrior's training included running races, wrestling, riding and archery. As a result he became tough, physically fit and self-reliant. He also learned how to put his trust in other members of the tribe or band, and to co-operate with other warriors.

Preparations for battle were carefully made by the leaders. When war was declared, all the warriors willing to fight smoked a ceremonial pipe, put on their ceremonial clothes, took up their weapons and performed a war dance.

COUNTING COUP

A warrior's bravery was not judged only by how many men he killed; far more courageous was 'counting coup'. This meant getting close enough to an armed enemy to be able to touch him with a hand or a 'coup stick' without actually harming him. 'Counting coup' showed that the warrior had risked great danger - greater than killing from a distance with an arrow or a gun. Counting coup was rewarded with special honours. When enemy warriors *were* killed, their scalps might be taken as trophies.

AFTER THE BATTLE

The return of a successful war party was cause for celebration. If scalps *had* been taken, Blackfoot warriors rode into camp with their faces painted black, carrying the scalps on long poles. A man who had led four war parties and gained distinction in all of them was awarded the great honour of becoming a 'shirtwearer'. He was presented with a specially painted shirt to proclaim his brave deeds.

SHIELDS AND BONNETS

Shields were an item of battledress with two important functions - to physically stop an arrow, and protect the owner with spiritual power. They were made from rawhide. They were decorated with claws and feathers, and painted with designs relating to his vision.

Shields and warbonnets were always prepared carefully before a battle. If they were misused, such as being dropped in mud, they had to be ceremonially purified before they could be used again.

FIREPOWER

When the settlers arrived, they taught the Indians to work metal. The traders also sold metal knives which soon replaced the traditional stone and bone tools and weapons. However, it was gunpowder and guns that transformed warfare on the Plains. The Indians bought guns from the traders and used them for killing buffalo - and, whenever necessary, their enemies.

Guns were treasured items, and, like bows, were carried in buckskin cases decorated with beadwork. However, the bow continued to be used long after the introduction of guns, because the early muskets were difficult to load on horseback, and could not be fired as quickly as arrows.

This pipe-tomahawk has a steel blade, made in Europe or North America. It could be used as an axe or a pipe. Traditionally, Plains Indians fought with bows and arrows, stone-headed clubs, spears and shields.

Sometimes a war party (above) would return from a raid with prisoners. Although captives were often mocked and tortured, they might also then be adopted as new members of the tribe.

The scalp dance (left) was performed to celebrate a victory in battle. The widows and other mourners of those who had lost their lives, and the female relatives of surviving warriors, took part. The warriors might be rewarded with feathers to wear.

39

TRADE

The see-through scene below shows a trading post in the mid-19th century. Each post was run by a manager and had quarters for visiting traders. The post was surrounded by a strong wooden wall, a palisade, and had blockhouses where people could shelter from an attack. Plains Indian bands sometimes set up camps near the forts, which were within easy reach of their territory.

Trading was always an important activity on the Great Plains. Long before the white man arrived, tribes traded with each other. Sometimes this was along trading routes that had been established thousands of years before by their ancestors. Villagers could offer corn, tobacco and other agricultural products to the more nomadic tribes. In exchange they got buffalo hides, flint knives and tools. Later they bought horses and guns from European traders.

EARLY CONTACTS

The white men who appeared on the Plains in the early 19th century were hunters, travellers and explorers. The Indians did not feel threatened by these few new arrivals. In return for their hides, furs and tobacco, the Indians traded for horses, metal tools, beads, calico (cotton cloth) and guns. European merchants soon found a ready market for the furs and skins in Britain, France, Spain and Russia. They founded companies like the American Fur Company, which set up trading posts such as Fort Clark (near the main Mandan village), Fort Union and Fort Laramie. These trading forts also served as outposts for the US Army.

SMITHS TRADING COMPANY

SLAUGHTER AND DECEPTION

The demand for furs and skins was enormous, and the companies did not just rely on the Indians to provide hides. They also sent trappers into the heart of Indian country to boost the supply. The whites took everything they wanted, without thought for the consequences. Between 1872 and 1874, over 3½ million buffalo were slaughtered. As a result, many of the buffalo herds were wiped out completely.

In some cases, the trade was fair and of benefit to both sides. But more often than not, the traders were dishonest. They cheated the Indians by using short measures, paying them a pittance for their hides. They also plied them with quantities of alcoholic spirits (called 'rot-gut'), which usually made the warriors very sick. After a heavy drinking session whole bands would be unable to hunt or provide for the needs of the tribe. Encouraged by the traders, some Indians gradually stopped providing food and clothing for themselves. Instead they began to rely on goods supplied at the trading posts.

Friend

Tipi

1 **Manager's house**
2 **Trading post shop**
3 **Storehouse**
4 **Quarters for visiting traders**
5 **Workshop**
6 **Brick chimney stack**
7 **Blockhouse**
8 **Palisade**
9 **Plains Indian camp**

Although the Plains peoples shared similar customs and beliefs, they spoke different languages and could not necessarily understand each other. Therefore a system of hand-signs evolved, similar to the sign languages used today by the deaf. The signs (above) were understood all over the Plains. Myths, exploits and trade deals could all be explained by signs.

SETTLERS AND INVADERS

I n 1843, gold was discovered in California, and the 'Gold Rush' began. Many new settlers flooded into the area, seeking land and wealth. They travelled in covered wagons across the lands of the Plains Indians, along the 'Oregon Trail'.

A NEW INVASION

The 'invaders' - the government, the settlers and the Christian missionaries - did not understand the Indians' way of life. They felt they had a natural superiority and a 'divine right' to conquer the Indians. They tried to stamp out traditional Indian culture and replace it with their own. Indian burial grounds were desecrated, and ceremonies such as the Sun Dance were made illegal.

As well as these problems, regular contact with the whites also brought diseases that were unknown to the peoples of the Plains. These included killer diseases such as smallpox, against which they had no resistance. The smallpox epidemic of 1837-38 killed all but 160 of the entire Mandan nation.

UNDER THREAT

The Indians tried to live in peace with the newcomers. The Indians believed that land was not owned, but held in a sacred trust, for the use and benefit of all. But the Europeans believed that all territory had its price and could be owned entirely by the purchaser. The Indians had a name for this kind of white man - *wasi'chu*, meaning literally 'one who takes the fat' or 'greedy person'.

As the whites claimed more of the richest lands and broke promises without apology, the Indians realised their way of life was under threat. Fighting broke out in various parts of the Plains. In the early 1860s, the government tried to develop the Bozeman Trail. This route led through the heart of Indian lands to the gold fields in the Rocky Mountains. When the government started building forts on the trail, the Oglala Sioux chief Red Cloud declared war.

The 'Battle of the Hundred Slain', as the Plains Indians called it, was the most important battle of Red Cloud's War. In 1866, a Captain Fetterman of the US Army boasted that he could ride through the whole Sioux nation with no more than 80 men. His entire command of 82 soldiers was then slaughtered by the Oglala Sioux, Cheyenne and Arapaho.

THE FORT LARAMIE TREATY

In what became known as 'Red Cloud's War', the Sioux chief won many small but important victories. The government was forced to negotiate the Fort Laramie Treaty of 1868. Under the terms of the treaty, the government abandoned its forts, and the Sioux were 'given' 50 million acres of land covering parts of Nebraska, Wyoming, Montana and North and South Dakota. The Treaty stated: 'No white person shall be permitted to settle upon any portion of the territory or, without the consent of the Indians, first had and obtained, to pass through same.'

However, the Treaty had not long been in effect when gold was discovered in the sacred Black Hills. The US Government tried to purchase the mountains, but Red Cloud insisted the land was not for sale. He demanded that the government respect and honour the treaty they had signed only eight years earlier.

'The white men have surrounded me and have left me nothing but an island. When we first had this land we were strong, now our nation is melting away like snow on the hillsides where the sun is warm; while the white people grow like blades of grass when summer is coming.'

— *Red Cloud* —

LITTLE BIG HORN

The government sent the Army to defend the gold prospectors and claim the hills. One of the army officers was General Custer, an ambitious young man who wanted to be a hero. In the Big Horn Mountains he found a large camp of Chief Sitting Bull's Sioux Indians gathered for their annual Sun Dance. Although his five troops of the 7th Cavalry were far outnumbered, he attacked them. The Battle of Little Big Horn, as it came to be known, was a great victory for the Sioux.

But nothing seemed to deter the invaders. The sale of the Black Hills was finally forced in 1876, and the Sioux lands were further reduced in size in 1879.

An Indian's representation of the Battle of the Little Big Horn. The great Sioux war leader, Chief Crazy Horse, can be seen in the centre.

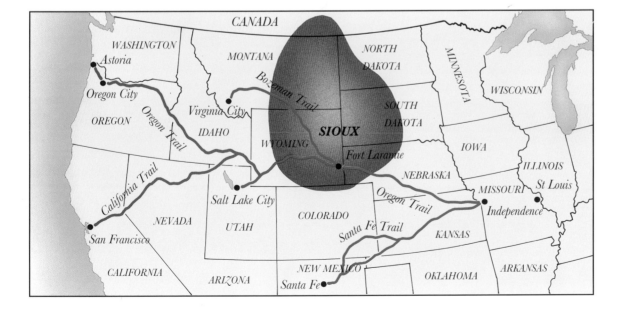

This map shows the main routes across Sioux lands. The tribes fought fiercely, but in vain, to keep a hold on their traditional homelands. They finally agreed to stay within a specified area, only to find that the area would be further diminished over the next 40 years.

43

THE RESERVATIONS

Below, this fanciful picture of the massacre of Sioux at Wounded Knee Creek in 1890 was first published in a newspaper. In fact, the band had very few, if any, weapons; the cavalry had rapid-firing Gatling guns. In the bottom photograph, Indians are cutting up a cattle carcass provided for food by the Reservation Agency.

By the end of the 1880s, many of the bands were so hard-pressed they had little choice but to surrender to the government. The government's solution to the 'Indian problem' was to divide up the tribes by putting them on reserved land, or reservations. Agents were appointed to manage the reservations, and to control the food supplies.

'CIVILIZATION'

The reservation Indians were looked on as 'wards' of the US government, who decided they needed to be 'civilized' at all costs. Their lives were totally controlled by their agent, appointed by the government in Washington. To the white man, long hair and traditional dress symbolized savagery. Reservation Indians had to wear European clothing, known as 'citizen dress'. Every Indian male had to cut his hair short and give up his braids.

The people were also forced to give up their tipis and earth lodges and live in wooden or log houses. Indian men had to become farmers, regardless of their traditional occupation. This was particularly insulting, since women had always done the farming on the Plains. In any case, the reservation land was usually of little value and interest to anyone else.

CHILDREN

Indian children were sent to school, often to boarding schools away from their parents and tribal influences. They were taken by force, given 'English' names and trained in the white man's ways. If they spoke in their own language they were beaten severely.

When they left school and went back to the reservation, these children felt out of place. But in white society they were refused good jobs and faced racial hatred. There was really no place they felt they belonged.

LAST RESISTANCE

By 1890 the Plains Indians were in a desperate state. Most tribes were starving. The government had cut off the food and clothing rations, and the first crops planted by order of the Reservation Agency had failed. In a last desperate attempt to stave off total defeat, the Ghost Dance movement swept the Plains. The movement called for the intervention of Wakan Tanka to drive out the whites and restore traditional ways of life. The settlers were frightened and called in the army.

This led to the final confrontation with the Sioux nation - the infamous massacre of Wounded Knee Creek. An Indian camp near Pine Ridge was surrounded by members of the 7th Cavalry, re-formed after Custer's defeat at the Little Big Horn. The troopers ordered the Indians to surrender their weapons. One of them went off, and the soldiers let loose volleys of shots and raked the tipis with their fire. When the shooting was over, nearly 300 of the 350-strong camp - consisting mainly of women and children - were dead.

INDIAN POWER

In spite of all the government's attempts, the native American people refused to vanish completely into the white man's culture. In the late 1960s, several new organizations, such as the National Indian Youth Council and the more militant American Indian Movement (AIM), urged Indians to be more forceful in seeking their economic and political rights. They pointed out that the Indians suffered poverty and injustice, both on the reservations and in the cities.

NEW PROTEST

Their campaigns got widespread support from around the world. In 1969 a group of Indians occupied the abandoned prison on the island of Alcatraz for 18 months. Then, in 1973, AIM occupied the village of Wounded Knee on the site of the 1890 massacre. They demanded the return of lands taken in violation of treaty agreements. Unfortunately many people were wounded and two Indians died in gun battles with the police.

The Indians also began legal action to recover land taken by the settlers. In 1980 the Sioux nation was awarded $122 million in payment for land seized illegally in the 1870s. However, no amount of money could properly compensate for the loss and destruction of their way of life. In spite of increasing interest and awareness of traditional Indian history and culture, life remains difficult and most First Americans feel confined to reservations.

Sitting Bull, a Sioux chief, led a last great gathering of Plains Indians against the US Army and settlers.

Two food ration tickets, issued to Indian families on reservations. These could be exchanged for weekly supplies of beef, flour, cornmeal, salt, coffee, sugar and soap.

The Ghost Dance ceremony, carried out according to the instructions of Wovoka, a Paiute prophet. Wovoka dreamt that the Great Mystery would save the Indian people and restore them to their former glory, if everyone performed this dance. Dancers sometimes wore special shirts that they believed would protect them from the white man's bullets.

KEY DATES AND GLOSSARY

This book tells how most Plains Indians lived in the early years of European settlement. Their way of life at this time lasted less than 300 years. After this, the Plains Indian nations were subjugated and many of their traditions destroyed.

c15,000 BC Paleo-Indians cross from Asia into North America and disperse across the continent.

1492 Columbus stumbles on America, expecting it to be Asia.

1541 Spaniard Francisco de Coronado makes what is probably the first contact with Plains Indians' culture.

1607 The English establish their first colony in Jamestown, Virginia.

c1800 American Fur Company sets up trading posts along Missouri River, deep into northern Plains territory.

1812 US government builds the first fort on the Plains, and signs peace treaties with local tribes.

1830s Plains now a centre of a booming trade in fur pelts and buffalo hides. George Catlin records the way of life in his paintings and journal. Karl Bodmer accompanies Prince

Maximilian on expedition to Plains.

1838 'Trail of Tears'. Cherokee Indians are forcibly moved from their homelands into Oklahoma.

1848 Gold discovered in California. Thousands of prospectors and settlers push westward.

1866 The Fetterman Fight.

1868 Fort Laramie Treaty.

1876 Battle of the Little Big Horn.

1887 Dawes Allotment Act attempts to divide reservation land into small plots owned by individual Indians (whether they consented or not).

1890 US troops massacre Sioux Indians at Wounded Knee, South Dakota.

1924 US citizenship granted to all Indians.

1934 Indian Reorganization Act reverses Dawes Allotment Act.

1953 Termination Act. Jurisdiction over Indian land passes from federal to state control.

1969 Indians occupy Alcatraz Island in the first modern Indian protest.

1972 A large convoy of cars drives across the US to petition the US government on Indian grievances.

1973 Members of the American Indian Movement (AIM) occupy the village of Wounded Knee.

Mandan Indians gather wood from the Missouri river during the spring thaw. Their village can be seen on the cliff in the background. A trading post has been built to the right of the village. This scene is based on paintings and sketches by Karl Bodmer, who described how the Mandan paddled their boats between the broken ice and even pulled a drowned elk from the freezing water.

Glossary

calumet: smoking pipe usually associated with rituals of peace, war and hunting, and often decorated with porcupine quills and feathers.

counting coup: method of gaining battle honours. Getting close to an enemy and touching him or standing face-to-face with him (as opposed to killing him) was considered an especially brave act.

moccasin: soft leather footwear, often lavishly decorated with beadwork.

parfleche: large rawhide container used for holding dried food or personal items.

reservation: area of land set apart for the Indians to live on at the end of the 19th century by the US government.

scalp: the skin covering a person's head where the hair grows. Warriors sometimes took the scalps of their enemies as trophies.

tipi: Plains Indian dwelling, consisting of a cone-shaped frame of poles covered with a buffalo-hide cover.

travois: an 'A' shaped wooden frame with two long poles and a crosspiece between. Pulled by a horse, a travois was used to transport a family's belongings. Earlier, smaller ones were pulled by dogs.

Wakan Tanka: Lakota Sioux term meaning 'The Creator', 'The Great Spirit' or 'The Great Mystery'.

wasi'chu: Lakota Sioux word meaning 'takes fat' or 'greedy person'. It was used to describe the white Europeans who overran the Plains in the 19th century.

wicasa wakan: Lakota Sioux term meaning 'man of mystery', referring to a person who calls upon the spiritual world for help to cure people or gain power or protection. These spiritual leaders are sometimes known as holy men or medicine men.

Quotations

Most of the quotations from this book are the words of Plains Indians themselves. Some are from the speeches of ancient leaders. They have been compiled in *Touch The Earth*, Garnstone Press, 1971, and *Bury My Heart At Wounded Knee*, by Dee Brown, Holt, Reinehart & Winston, New York 1971. Lame Deer was a contemporary Sioux *wicasa wakan* who told his life story to Richard Erdoes, published in *Lame Deer: Seeker of Visions*. Quotations by non-Indians include that by Prince Maximilian, a German traveller who wrote an account of his expedition, *Journey into the North American Interior 1832-34*, and Edward Curtis, a photographer and writer who spent most of his life compiling a 20-volume work, *The North American Indian*, which was finally completed in 1930. Artists George Catlin and Karl Bodmer visited the Plains in the 1830s. They observed and recorded the way of life of many Plains Indian tribes.

INDEX

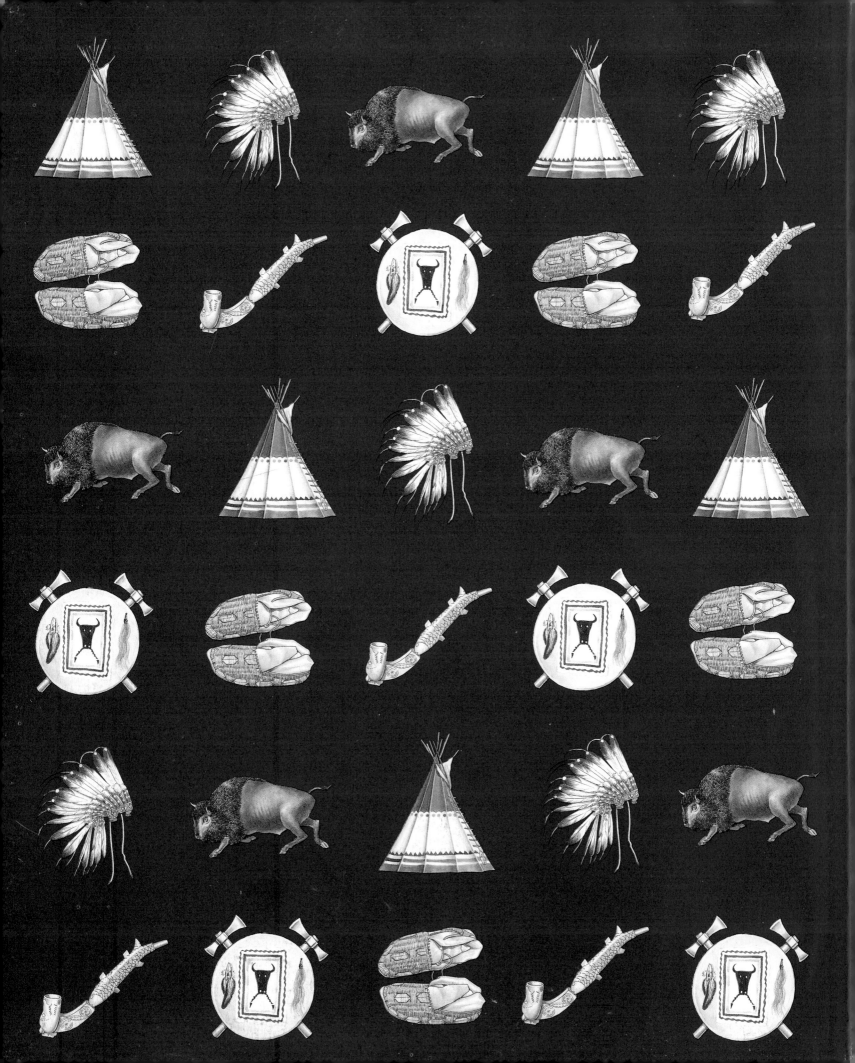